Susie Mountain is a solicitor-advocate, an accredited specialist in Family Law and a trained collaborative practitioner. Susie is based in Aberdeen, but regularly appears in courts (including the Court of Session) across the country. She has particular expertise in cross border/international family law cases, child relocations and cohabitation cases (relating both to claims on separation and claims on death). Susie is a member of the Family Law Association (FLA) and of Consensus. Susie is passionate about educating younger lawyers entering the profession and frequently delivers seminars both in person and online.

Donna McKay is a solicitor. She is accredited by the Law Society of Scotland as a family law mediator, as a specialist in family law and as a specialist in child law. She is also an experienced Collaborative lawyer. Donna has over 20 years of experience in family law. Donna has a particular interest and expertise in child law including child relocation cases, contact/residence disputes and adoptions. She also has experience in complex financial provision cases. Donna is skilled in traditional negotiation and is an accomplished litigator. Donna sits on the Board of the North East charity "Avenue" (providing services such as mediation, supported/supervised contact and counselling) and is the chair of the local pod of Consensus (North East Scotland pod). She is a member of: Family Law Association (FLA); Comprehensive Accredited Lawyer Mediators (CALM); and Consensus.

Ken MacDonald is a leading disputes lawyer with 30 years' experience. He is dual qualified in English and in Scots law and is Head of International Arbitration at Brodies LLP. Ken has been involved in the handling of disputes through negotiation, mediation, arbitration, expert determination, international arbitration and litigation with a view to securing expeditious resolution or avoidance of disputes. He attained the Diploma in International Dispute Resolution (Arbitration) with merit from Queen Mary University of London. He is a former President of The Society of Advocates in Aberdeen.

A Practical Guide to International Issues for Scottish Family Lawyers

A Practical Guide to International Issues for Scottish Family Lawyers

Susie Mountain

Partner & Solicitor Advocate, Brodies LLP

MA (Hons) LLB DipLP NP

Donna McKay

Legal Director, Brodies LLP

LLB (Hons) DipLP NP

Ken MacDonald,

Partner, Brodies LLP

LLB (Hons) DipLP NP

Law Brief Publishing

Published 2024 by Law Brief Publishing, an imprint of Law Brief Publishing Ltd
30 The Parks
Minehead
Somerset
TA24 8BT

www.lawbriefpublishing.com

Paperback: 978-1-913715-82-3

PREFACE

The arrival of Covid-19 had a significant impact on the work of family lawyers. For those of us involved in cases with an international element, the effects were keenly felt. Whilst travel was severely restricted, contact arrangements for children were in disarray and often hotly disputed.

The impact on the economy forced a new wave of relocation as people migrated for work. This had an inevitable knock-on effect on personal relationships, with the result being that law firms throughout Scotland saw an uptick in instructions where cross jurisdictional advice was required.

This practical guide explores the key elements for Scots family law practitioners to consider in cases with an international dimension. We cover matters relating to the construction of relationships, resolving issues on separation and difficulties relating to arrangements for children. We also take a look at how clients can seek to future proof themselves in a world where global mobility is on the rise.

The law in this book is correct, to the best of our knowledge, as at 13 December 2023.

Susie Mountain,
Donna McKay,
Ken MacDonald,
December 2023

CONTENTS

CHAPTER ONE

RELATIONSHIPS ENTERED INTO ABROAD

Formal requirements: marriage

Preparing for a "wedcation" requires more than simply packing a suitcase. The requirements for British nationals who wish to marry in other jurisdictions differ significantly from country to country. A breakdown by each individual country can be found on the website of the Foreign and Commonwealth Office[1]. Consulates or Embassies can also provide the relevant information. The main thing to bear in mind is that in many countries it is necessary to provide a "certificate of no impediment" prior to marrying. These can be obtained from most Registry offices and are valid for only three months from the date of issue. Translations of any legal documents may also be required, so clients who are considering entering into foreign nuptials will need to be mindful of timescales.

As to whether a marriage entered into overseas will be legally recognised in Scotland, the relevant legislation is section 38 of the Family Law (Scotland) Act 2006, which is in the following terms:

> "*Validity of marriages*
>
> *(1) Subject to the Foreign Marriage Act 1892 (c. 23), the question whether a marriage is formally valid shall be*

[1] https://www.gov.uk/marriage-abroad

determined by the law of the place where the marriage was celebrated.

(2) The question whether a person who enters into a marriage—

(a) had capacity; or

(b) consented,

to enter into it shall, subject to subsections (3) and (4) and to section 50 of the Family Law Act 1986 (c. 55) (non-recognition of divorce or annulment in another jurisdiction no bar to remarriage), be determined by the law of the place where, immediately before the marriage, that person was domiciled.

(3) If a marriage entered into in Scotland is void under a rule of Scots internal law, then, notwithstanding subsection (2), that rule shall prevail over any law under which the marriage would be valid.

(4) The capacity of the person to enter into the marriage shall not be determined under the law of the place where, immediately before the marriage, the person was domiciled in so far as it would be contrary to public policy in Scotland for such capacity to be so determined.

(5) If the law of the place in which a person is domiciled requires a person under a certain age to obtain parental consent before entering into a marriage, that requirement shall not be taken to affect the capacity of a person to enter into a marriage in Scotland unless failure to obtain such consent would render invalid any marriage that the person purported to enter into in any form anywhere in the world."

It is therefore important that parties to overseas marriages check the following:

1. Did the marriage take place in accordance with the law and customs of the country in which the parties were married – i.e. was a legal and binding marriage created?

2. Is the marriage contrary to Scottish public policy?

3. Do they have their marriage certificate? Clients would be well advised to ensure that they have their marriage certificate (and ideally, also a translated version where necessary). In the event of a future separation, obtaining certificates from overseas can create long delays.

Registration of marriage ceremony conducted overseas

Clients often assume that their marriage needs to be formally registered in Scotland in order to be legally recognised on Scottish soil. Marriages conducted overseas cannot, in fact, be registered in Scotland.

Lex loci celebrationis

What happens if there is a question mark over where the marriage took place? This was the case in *A v K*[2]. The judgment in that case is well worth a read, as it provides a useful overview of the key case law. The pursuer in *A v K* was a UK national of Pakistani heritage. At the age of twenty she had entered into a marriage with a national of Pakistan who she had met online. She had not met him in person at any time before, during or after the marriage ceremony. The marriage took place by telephone. During the marriage ceremony, which was conducted by a priest, the pursuer was in Scotland. Her fiancé was in Pakistan. After the ceremony, a marriage certificate was sent to the pursuer, which she duly signed and

2 *A v K* (2011) SLT 873

send to the Pakistan Consulate in Glasgow. The action for declarator of nullity was not defended. Notwithstanding that, after requesting further information, Lord Stewart was not persuaded that the marriage took place partly in Scotland, but instead found that it took place wholly in Pakistan. It was held that, as the telephone ceremony created a valid contract of marriage under the law of Pakistan, the marriage ought to be considered valid by the Scottish court.

Civil partnerships

As with marriage, the requirements for parties seeking to enter into a civil partnership overseas are helpfully spelled out by the FCO website.

So, for example, the website states that same or mixed sex couples can enter into a civil partnership in Austria after first providing a certificate of no impediment. This may need to be an exchanged for a similar certificate with validity in Austria. It may also need to be legalised and translated. By contrast, in Azerbaijan it is not possible to enter into a civil partnership and therefore any purported civil partnership stated to have taken in place in Azerbaijan would not be accepted as valid in Scotland.

The applicable legislation for civil partnerships entered into overseas is section 215 of the Civil Partnership Act 2004, the general rule of which is as follows:

> *(1) Two people are to be treated as having formed a civil partnership as a result of having registered an overseas relationship if, under the relevant law, they—*
>
> > *(a) had capacity to enter into the relationship, and*
> >
> > *(b) met all requirements necessary to ensure the formal validity of the relationship.*

The "relevant law" in this regard is the law of the country in which the civil partnership was entered into.

Cohabitants

One useful quirk of the provisions for cohabitants set out within the Family Law (Scotland) Act 2006 is that there is no stipulation that the cohabitation must have taken place in Scotland in order for a claim to be made in terms of section 28 (claims on separation) or section 29 (claims on death). There is therefore no requirement to have "formal recognition" of a cohabitation which took place overseas, although other provisions regarding domicile may apply.

Clients should be aware, however, that few countries worldwide have specific protections in place for those in cohabiting relationships. Although it is likely to be possible to make a claim in Scotland in the event of either party to the relationship being Scottish domiciled, there may not be the option to make a claim in any other jurisdiction. Some countries require a minimum period of cohabitation, or for the cohabitation to be formally registered in that country, before any claim can be made. If clients are seeking advice prior to a move abroad, it is important, from a risk management perspective, to canvass these issues with them.

CHAPTER TWO

JURISDICTION ON SEPARATION: SCOTLAND

Choice of jurisdiction

Parties will often have a choice of jurisdiction on divorce or dissolution of civil partnership. For risk management purposes, advisors should ascertain firstly whether there is more than one jurisdiction in which a claim might competently be made; and if so, in which jurisdiction their client is likely to achieve the most favourable outcome. This investigative work should be carried out before any steps are taken such as writing to the other party, or raising court proceedings. It is, of course, possible, although undesirable, to have litigation ongoing in more than one jurisdiction in relation to the same matter. It is crucial to emphasise here that there can be an astronomical divergence in the way that different countries deal with financial provision on divorce.

If it becomes apparent that there may be a choice of jurisdiction, the client should be given a broad overview of the way in which the law would apply to their circumstances in Scotland. They should also be advised to consult a lawyer in the other applicable jurisdiction(s) and to do so on an urgent basis. It is often easiest for these discussions to take place between the two solicitors directly to ensure that the correct information is obtained.

Jurisdiction on divorce

It is often thought that parties need to divorce in the country in which they were married. This is not necessarily the case.

Jurisdiction on divorce in Scotland is governed by the Divorce and Matrimonial Proceedings Act 1973 (DMPA), in section 7 (2A) (Court of Session actions) and section 8 (2) (Sheriff Court actions). Scottish courts will have jurisdiction to deal with a divorce (regardless of where the marriage took place) if (and only if) either party to the marriage:

(a) is domiciled in Scotland on the date when the action is begun, or

(b) was habitually resident in Scotland throughout the period of one year ending with that date.

This means that it is possible for a divorce to be dealt with in Scotland, even if neither party remains living in Scotland, provided that one party has Scottish domicile.

These jurisdictional rules apply equally to same and mixed sex couples, as the Family Law Regulations[3] revoked the Marriage (Same Sex Couples) (Jurisdiction and Recognition of Judgments) (Scotland) Regulations 2014 and amended Schedule 1 of the DMPA to bring this into line.

---

[3] *Jurisdiction and Judgments (Family, Civil Partnership and Marriage (Same Sex Couples)) (EU Exit) (Scotland) (Amendment etc) Regulations 2019 (SSI 2019/104)*

Jurisdiction on dissolution of civil partnership

The Family Law Regulations amended section 225 of the Civil Partnership Act 2004, so that Scotland now has jurisdiction to deal with dissolution of civil partnership on the same bases as for divorce (either party being Scottish domiciled or habitually resident in Scotland for a period of one year). If neither of those apply, it may still be possible to make an application for dissolution in the Court of Session in terms of section 225 (1) (c) provided that the following conditions are met:

(i) *the two people concerned registered as civil partners of each other in Scotland,*

(ii) no court has, or is recognised as having, jurisdiction, and

(iii) it appears to the court to be in the interests of justice to assume jurisdiction in the case."

Jurisdiction for cohabitation claims

In terms of section 28 (9) of the Family Law Scotland Act 2006, the correct court to determine a financial claim on separation would be the court that would be entitled to deal with an application for divorce or dissolution. The quirk of this for cohabitants is that a financial claim can be made in Scotland on separation even if the parties have lived outside Scotland for the entire duration of the cohabitation. This is potentially useful given that protection for cohabitants is not available in all jurisdictions.

Can a claim in Scotland be entertained after divorce/dissolution has been effected in another jurisdiction?

A financial claim can be entertained under Scots Law after the granting of divorce or dissolution of civil partnership in another jurisdiction, but only in certain circumstances. The relevant legislative provision can be found at section 28 of the Matrimonial and Family Proceedings Act 1984, which provides that Scottish courts may entertain applications for financial provision after overseas divorce provided that certain jurisdictional requirements and certain conditions are met. The jurisdictional requirements are as follows:

a) The applicant was domiciled or habitually resident in Scotland on the date the application was made; and

b) the other party to the marriage was domiciled or habitually resident in Scotland on the date the application was made; or that was the case when the parties last lived together as husband and wife; or

c) on the date the application was made, was an owner or tenant of, or had a beneficial interest in, property in Scotland which had at some time been a matrimonial home of the parties; and

d) (for a sheriff court action), one of the parties was, at the date of the application, habitually resident in the sheriffdom; or one of the parties was an owner or tenant of, or had a beneficial interest in, property in Scotland which had at some time been a matrimonial home of the parties.

Accordingly, this legislation only applies in fairly narrow circumstances.

The conditions are as follows:

(i) The divorce is recognised in Scotland;

(ii) The *other party* to the marriage initiated the divorce proceedings (so your client must have been the defender in the action);

(iii) The application was made within 5 years after the date when the divorce took effect;

(iv) A court in Scotland would have jurisdiction to entertain an action for divorce between the parties if such an action had been brought in Scotland immediately before the foreign divorce took effect;

(v) The marriage had a substantial connection with Scotland; and

(vi) Both parties are living at the time of the application.

Section 29 sets out broadly how the section 28 provisions might be applied:

> *(1) Subject to subsections (2) to (5) below, Scots law shall apply, with any necessary modifications, in relation to an application under section 28 above as it would apply if the application were being made in an action for divorce in Scotland.*
>
> *(2) In disposing of an application entertained by it under the said section 28, the court shall exercise its powers so as to place the parties, in so far as it is reasonable and practicable to do so, in the financial position in which they would have been if the application had been disposed of, in an action for divorce in Scotland, on the date on which the foreign divorce took effect.*
>
> *(3) In determining what is reasonable and practicable for the purposes of subsection (2) above, the court shall have regard in particular to—*

(a) the parties' resources, present and foreseeable at the date of disposal of the application;

(b) any order made by a foreign court in or in connection with the divorce proceedings for the making of financial provision in whatever form, or the transfer of property, by one of the parties to the other; and

(c) subsection (5) below.

(4) Except where subsection (5) below applies, the court may make an order for an interim award of a periodical allowance where—

(a) it appears from the applicant's averments that in the disposal of the application an order for financial provision is likely to be made; and

(b) the court considers that such an interim award is necessary to avoid hardship to the applicant.

(5) Where but for section 28(2)(b)(iii) above the court would not have jurisdiction to entertain the application, the court may make an order—

(a) relating to the former matrimonial home or its furniture and plenishings; or

(b) that the other party to the marriage shall pay to the applicant a capital sum not exceeding the value of that other party's interest in the former matrimonial home and its furniture and plenishings,

but shall not be entitled to make any other order for financial provision.

The same now applies on the dissolution of civil partnerships abroad.

In terms of case law dealing with this issue, the case of *Tahir* is worth a look. *Tahir v Tahir*[4] was an Outer House appeal in which a lady who had been divorced in Pakistan sought various ancillary orders on her return to Scotland. Mrs Tahir had raised a divorce action in Scotland prior to the Pakistan divorce being granted. Her Scottish action continued post-divorce. She sought a capital sum payment and various ancillary orders. The court had no difficulty in making such orders based on the provisions of the Act.

4 *Tahir v Tahir* 1993 SLT 194

CHAPTER THREE

JURISDICTION ON SEPARATION: UK AND THE CHANNEL ISLANDS

Special provisions apply in Scotland where a competing consistorial action (that is to say, an action of divorce, separation, declarator of marriage or declarator of nullity of marriage) is raised in one of the following "related jurisdictions": England & Wales, Northern Ireland, Jersey (including Alderney and Sark), Guernsey and the Isle of Man.

Section 8 of Schedule 3 to the Domicile and Matrimonial Proceedings Act 1983 ("the 1973 Act") provides the following:

> *Where before the beginning of the proof in any action for divorce which is continuing in the Court of Session or in the Sheriff Court it appears to the Court concerned on the application of a party to the marriage—*
>
> *(a) that in respect of the same marriage proceedings for divorce or nullity of marriage are continuing in a related jurisdiction; and*
>
> *(b) that the parties to the marriage have resided together after the marriage was contracted; and*
>
> *(c) that the place where they resided together when the action in the Court was begun or, if they did not then reside together, where they last resided together before the date on which that action was begun is in that jurisdiction; and*

> *(d) that either of the said parties was habitually resident in that jurisdiction throughout the year ending with the date on which they last resided together before the date on which that action was begun; it shall be the duty of the Court, subject to paragraph 10(2) below, to sist the action before it.*

The operative word here is "duty". The court does not have a choice but to sist the Scottish proceedings in these circumstances; a sist is mandatory. This can, of course, lead to the question of where the parties did, in fact, last live together being hotly disputed. The question can be difficult to determine in matters where parties have spent time living between homes in different jurisdictions. This may well necessitate a preliminary proof on that issue.

CHAPTER FOUR

RAISING AN ACTION IN SCOTLAND: WHICH COURT?

Having established that your client has jurisdiction to raise an action in Scotland and a court action being necessary for whatever reason, the question turns to whether to raise such an action in the Sheriff Court or the Court of Session.

Court of Session

The Court of Session has jurisdiction in relation to consistorial actions in terms of section 7 of the Domicile and Matrimonial Proceedings Act 1973 ("the 1973 Act").

Divorce

The Court of Session has jurisdiction to deal with a divorce case where either party to the marriage is Scottish domiciled; or either party was habitually resident in Scotland for a period of one year prior to the action being raised.

Declarator of marriage

The Court of Session has jurisdiction in relation to a declarator of marriage where either party to the marriage is Scottish domiciled; or either part was habitually resident in Scotland for a period of one year prior to the action being raised; *or* either party died prior to the action being raised and was either Scottish domiciled at the date of death or had been habitually resident in Scotland for one year prior to the date of death. The same applies to declarators of nullity of marriage.

Sheriff Court

Divorce

The Sheriff Court has jurisdiction to deal with a divorce case where the domicile or one year habitual residence criteria are met (as in the Court of Session). In addition, either party to the marriage must have been resident in the Sheriffdom for a period of forty days prior to the action being raised; or for a period of not less than forty days ending not more than forty days before the date of the raising of the action, and has no known residence as at that date.

Declarator of marriage

The Sheriff Court has jurisdiction to deal with declarators of marriage or nullity of marriage on the same basis as those dealt with in the Court of Session, but with the additional Sheriff Court residence criteria also being met.

CHAPTER FIVE

BREXIT

It is fair to say that advising on separation and divorce post Brexit is not something that fills most Scottish family lawyers with delight. However, advising on separation and divorce post Brexit is something that we are now doing every day and this book would not be complete without a nod to the changes brought about by our exit from the EU.

History

The UK had been part of the EU and the European Community (its predecessor), since 1973, but the UK voted to depart the EU on 23 June 2016. On 29 March 2017 Article 50 was triggered, which put the UK on a two-year countdown to Brexit. Article 50 was then extended on more than one occasion.

The Withdrawal Agreement was agreed on 17 October 2019 and came into force on 1 February 2020. The UK left the EU and entered the "transition period" at 11pm on 31 January 2020. During that period, attention was given to what arrangements could be put into place between the UK and the EU for certain legal matters. All of this was happening, of course, whilst we were conducting our business from the cocoons of our homes, rather distracted by *another* significant world event. The important thing for our purposes is that no agreement was ultimately reached regarding arrangements for family law matters.

To ensure that there was provision in place in the event of a lack of agreement on family law matters by the end of the transition period,

Scotland enacted the Family Law Regulations[5] (FLR), which came into force on 3 December 2020.

The transition period then ended on 11pm on 31 December 2020.

Jurisdiction

Despite the fact that we are all advising on "separation post Brexit" on a regular basis, many cases on a typical family lawyer's desk will be straightforward in terms of jurisdiction. However, it is crucial from a risk management perspective to make sure that you have properly ruled jurisdictional considerations in or out before dispensing advice.

Pre Brexit, the key legislation governing divorce and separation in Scotland was set out in Brussels IIa (aka Brussels revised). The same was true for all other Member States, with the exception of Denmark. Article 3 of Brussels revised deals with jurisdiction for divorce, legal separation or marriage annulment and reads as follows:

> *Article 3* ***General jurisdiction***
>
> 1. *In matters relating to divorce, legal separation or marriage annulment, jurisdiction shall lie with the courts of the Member State*
>
>   *(a) in whose territory:*
>
>   - *the spouses are habitually resident, or*

5 *Jurisdiction and Judgments (Family, Civil Partnership and Marriage (Same Sex Couples)) (EU Exit) (Scotland) (Amendment etc) Regulations 2019 (SSI 2019/104)*

- *the spouses were last habitually resident, insofar as one of them still resides there, or*

- *the respondent is habitually resident, or*

- *in the event of a joint application, either of the spouses is habitually resident, or*

- *the applicant is habitually resident if he or she resided there for at least a year immediately before the application was made, or*

- *the applicant is habitually resident if he or she resided there for at least six months immediately before the application was made and is either a national of the Member State in question or, in the case of the United Kingdom and Ireland, has his or her 'domicile' there;*

(b) *of the nationality of both spouses or, in the case of the United Kingdom and Ireland, of the 'domicile' of both spouses.*

2. *For the purpose of this Regulation, 'domicile' shall have the same meaning as it has under the legal systems of the United Kingdom and Ireland.*

The sole reason for highlighting the point in this book is that these jurisdictional rules continue to apply to any actions raised prior to the end of the transition period (11pm on 31 December 2020). Such actions will gradually peter out as they draw to a conclusion, rather than there being a definitive line in the sand.

Of course, the provisions in Article 3 meant that it was certainly possible that more than one Member State might have jurisdiction to deal with a separation or divorce. Article 19 dealt with such a scenario through the avenue of the all important "*lis pendens*" rule, which reads as follows:

> 1. *Where proceedings relating to divorce, legal separation or marriage annulment between the same parties are brought before courts of different Member States, the court second seised shall of its own motion stay its proceedings until such time as the jurisdiction of the court first seised is established.*
>
> 2. *Where proceedings relating to parental responsibility relating to the same child and involving the same cause of action are brought before courts of different Member States, the court second seised shall of its own motion stay its proceedings until such time as the jurisdiction of the court first seised is established.*
>
> 3. *Where the jurisdiction of the court first seised is established, the court second seised shall decline jurisdiction in favour of that court.*

So, in a nutshell, this was a race to court. This prompted many missed nights of sleep in order to get actions warranted and served. The rationale behind this was to prevent the expense and complexity of having litigation ongoing in two different jurisdictions.

In Scotland, the Marriage (Same Sex Couples) (Jurisdiction and Recognition of Judgments) (Scotland) regulations 2014 and Civil Partnership Act 2004 and Civil Partnership (Jurisdiction of Judgments) (Scotland) Regulations 2005 regulated jurisdiction for same sex couples and civil partners, putting in place the same jurisdictional requirements.

Maintenance

The EU Maintenance Regulation is the somewhat catchier title of the Regulation otherwise known as "Council Regulation (EC) 4/2009 on jurisdiction, applicable law, recognition and enforcement of decisions and co-operation in matters relating to maintenance obligations". This regulation, which applied to the UK (including Scotland, of course), pre Brexit, governed recognition and enforcement. The maintenance regulation continues to apply to cases commenced prior to the end of the transition period (11pm on 31 December 2020).

Maintenance, in terms of Article 1 of the Maintenance Regulation, applies to "maintenance obligations arising from a family relationship, parentage, marriage or affinity." So for Scots Law purposes, we would be looking at standalone actions for aliment.

Prior to Brexit, in terms of Article 3 of the Maintenance Regulations, jurisdiction for maintenance actions was as follows:

In matters relating to maintenance obligations in Member States, jurisdiction shall lie with:

(a) the court for the place where the defendant is habitually resident, or

(b) the court for the place where the creditor is habitually resident, or

(c) the court which, according to its own law, has jurisdiction to entertain proceedings concerning the status of a person if the matter relating to maintenance is ancillary to those proceedings, unless that jurisdiction is based solely on the nationality of one of the parties, or

(d) the court which, according to its own law, has jurisdiction to entertain proceedings concerning parental responsibility

> *if the matter relating to maintenance is ancillary to those proceedings, unless that jurisdiction is based solely on the nationality of one of the parties.*

As with jurisdiction on divorce, this provision meant that it was of course possible for more than one Member State to have jurisdiction. In that event, the lis pendens rule would apply by virtue of Article 12, so the court first seised would take priority and the action second seised would be "stayed".

The other main implication of the EU maintenance regulation pre-Brexit was that it provided a mechanism for any maintenance decision made in Scotland to be recognised and enforced in other EU Member States, and vice versa. This no longer applies.

CHAPTER SIX

CONTEST OF JURISDICTION

In the event of competing actions being raised between Scotland and any other country, either party to the action may seek a discretionary sist of the Scottish proceedings in terms of section 3 of the Domicile and Matrimonial Proceedings Act 1984, which reads as follows:

> *9(1) Where before the beginning of the proof in any consistorial action which is continuing in the Court of Session or in a sheriff court, it appears to the court concerned—*
>
> *(a) that any other proceedings in respect of the marriage in question or capable of affecting its validity are continuing in another jurisdiction, and*
>
> *(b) that the balance of fairness (including convenience) as between the parties to the marriage is such that it is appropriate for those other proceedings to be disposed of before further steps are taken in the action in the said court,*
>
> *the court may then if it thinks fit sist that action.*
>
> *(2) In considering the balance of fairness and convenience for the purposes of sub-paragraph (1)(b) above, the court shall have regard to all factors appearing to be relevant, including the convenience of witnesses and any delay or expense which may result from the proceedings being sisted, or not being sisted.*

The Scottish court therefore has *discretion* to determine whether or not to sist the Scottish action, based on the test of fairness and convenience to the parties. This is the same whether the competing action is in an EU member state or any other international jurisdiction. However, it is critical to bear in mind that courts in other countries may not take the same view. Some jurisdictions may ignore competing proceedings altogether; or may have their own domestic rules stating that where an action is raised in a different jurisdiction, the action raised first should proceed. For that reason, obtaining early legal advice in any other countries which may have jurisdiction remains key.

CHAPTER SEVEN

PROTECTION: PRE AND POST NUPTIALS AND OTHER FORMS OF AGREEMENT

Pre-nuptial and post-nuptial agreements are generally considered to be binding in Scotland. Where there is an international dimension to a couple's relationship, it is crucial that advice is obtained in each country which may have, or may come to have, jurisdiction. Of course, knowing which country or countries may become relevant cannot always be predicted. For that reason, clients should be advised to re-visit any pre or post-nuptial agreements in the event of any significant life change (including a move overseas).

Prorogating jurisdiction

If Scotland is the preferred jurisdiction to deal with any dispute between the parties, it is worth including a clause to prorogate jurisdiction to Scotland. That will give an individual the best possible security regarding how matters will be determined in the event of a future permanent separation, even if they are residing out-with Scotland. Such a clause will not always be recognised or upheld by the country in which a divorce action is raised (out-with Scotland), so you cannot provide your client with any guarantees. In certain jurisdictions a domestic court may determine that it has jurisdiction and may in that event be prepared to deal with matters regardless of any election of jurisdiction. That being said, if a pre-nuptial agreement provides protection to both parties, this may guide the parties themselves to adhere to the terms of that pre-nuptial agreement and to deal with matters under Scots Law in the event of a marital breakdown.

Significant expense can be incurred where a pre-nuptial or post-nuptial agreement entered into in a different jurisdiction is contested, as any question as to the interpretation or validity of the agreement may require evidence from lawyers in the country in which the agreement was drafted.

Cohabitation agreements are of course also possible (and generally considered to be binding, at least by the Scottish courts). The fact that such an agreement is in existence is generally enough to persuade an errant cohabitant to comply. As previously indicated it does not matter, under Scots Law, if the parties did not spend the entirety of their cohabitation in Scotland in order for a 2006 Act claim to be made. The "appropriate court" for such an application is "the court which would have jurisdiction to hear an action of divorce/dissolution of civil partnership were [the parties] married or in a civil partnership." So, if the parties could legitimately divorce in Scotland, they could legitimately make a 2006 Act claim here.

Counter signing

When clients enter into Minutes of Agreement (whether pre-nuptial, post-nuptial or separation agreements) and one of them is living overseas, it is possible to sign the Agreements in counterpart. This allows the agreement to be signed as two separate copies which are then registered together in the Books of Council and Session. This avoids the delay which might otherwise be incurred by the passing of a single document back and forth overseas. It was previously thought that in Scotland counterpart signing was not competent. However, the brief piece of legislation known as The Legal Writings (Counterparts and Delivery) (Scotland) Act 2015 came into force on 1 July 2015 and put this matter beyond any doubt.

Mirror agreements

When parties have ties to more than one jurisdiction and there is the possibility that they may reside in several countries during their marriage; or where they have separated and are seeking to enter into a binding agreement, it may be advisable for them to sign 'mirror agreements'. This will involve the parties entering separate agreements under the laws of each jurisdiction to ensure that the contracts have the best prospect of being adhered to in the event of contest in any of the possible jurisdictions. This reinforces the requirement to obtain advice from lawyers in the various jurisdictions to which the parties are linked at an early opportunity.

CHAPTER EIGHT

ARBITRATION

Whilst it is fair to say that arbitration has not fully evolved in Scotland as a means of dispute resolution in family law matters it is apt for consideration as an effective route for achieving a binding determination in many of the challenges facing parties.

Arbitration of family law disputes is promoted by various stakeholders in Scotland including the Family Law Arbitration Group Scotland (known as FLAGS).

What is arbitration?

There are several definitions of arbitration.[6] They all have in common the concept of a referral by parties to a decision maker who pronounces a binding decision. Perhaps the simplest definition is that arbitration is a legally binding process where an independent third party is appointed to resolve the issues between parties.

To arbitrate there must be a contractual agreement between parties to refer their dispute to arbitration. This will usually happen where a contract (e.g., pre-nuptial agreement, cohabitation agreement etc) contains an agreement to arbitrate expressed in an arbitral clause. If there is no pre-existing contract, or no pre-existing contract providing for arbitration, parties can still choose to enter a contract to refer their dispute to arbitration.

6 See for example Lew et al., Comparative International Commercial Arbitration (2003), para 1-5.

Arbitration can be domestic or international.

A domestic arbitration can involve parties based in the same jurisdiction with agreement to their dispute being resolved by arbitration seated in the same jurisdiction. The seat of the arbitration is a legal concept and is distinguishable from the place where arbitration hearings take place. The seat of the arbitration determines the procedural law applicable to the arbitration and therefore matters concerning how the arbitration will be conducted. This can be a different law from the substantive law (of the contract) determining the rights and duties of the parties. It is generally preferable, though not essential, for the procedural law and the substantive law to be the same.

There is no overarching agreement for defining international arbitration. An international arbitration can involve parties based in different jurisdictions with agreement to their dispute being resolved by arbitration in the seat of either or neither of them. Both domestic and international arbitrations have commonality in that each reject (to the extent permissible) resort to the national courts for determination of their dispute and thus look to a resolution that goes beyond the domestic court sphere. Parties contract out of the national court system – the more usual route for settling family law disputes.

Advantages of arbitration

The process is flexible and enables the selection of a decision-maker with genuine expertise in the subject matter of the dispute. The process is private (and in most jurisdictions offers a considerable degree of confidentiality). It offers a quicker route to certainty and finality than litigation. Courts in many jurisdictions (and certainly in Scotland, and in England and Wales) are pro-arbitration and will not readily interfere with the decision of an arbitrator. There is therefore significantly less prospect of an appeal against an arbitral award being successfully taken. Arbitral appeals are dealt with by courts having jurisdiction in the seat of the arbitration.

Though less of an issue in family law cases, cost recoverability from the opposing party is better in arbitration than litigation with significantly higher rates of recovery of actual expenditure achievable. Crucially, arbitral awards are more readily enforceable around the world than court judgements. This is addressed in the chapter on Enforcement.

Arbitration should be given serious consideration in circumstances where parties would find themselves in the national courts of a jurisdiction with which they (and their advisers) are unfamiliar or uncomfortable. In that situation arbitration offers a solution to level the playing field in a way that litigation just does not allow. It should certainly be considered where the party the practitioner represents is likely to receive a financial payment from the other party where that other party resides in a jurisdiction that does not allow, or readily allow, the recognition and enforcement of court judgments from the national court that would otherwise have jurisdiction.

Disadvantages of arbitration

Time is required to appoint the arbitrator whose power comes from the arbitration agreement in the contract between parties. Whilst emergency arbitrators can be appointed in certain circumstances, courts are generally better at providing immediate interim remedies.

There is no real provision for summary determination or default judgment. Accordingly, where the opponent party chooses not to actively participate in the arbitration, there is still a requirement for the other party to present their case to a conclusion.

Use of Arbitration

For arbitration to be used (and thus for the jurisdiction of courts to be ousted) it must be provided for in a contract between parties. Alternatively, it is possible for parties to agree post-dispute to refer the issue to arbitration. Clearly, it is much easier to proceed to arbitration if this choice has been selected pre-dispute.

Arbitration is suitable for resolving many (though not all) family law disputes. Examples of suitable disputes include determination of (i) the valuation of matrimonial assets; (ii) the date of separation of parties; (iii) aliment; (iv) claims arising from a cohabitation agreement; (v) claims arising from pre-nuptial agreements; (vi) claims arising from post-nuptial agreements; and (vii) claims arising from separation agreements. Arbitration can be used to determine discrete issues within a wider range of disputes.

Certain family law disputes are however non-arbitrable. They cannot be competently referred to arbitration and any purported arbitral award would be unenforceable. Examples of such disputes include (i) declarator of parentage; (ii) dissolution; (iii) annulment; and (iv) divorce. Such matters determining the status of individuals where declaratory remedies are needed are within the province of courts and not arbitrators.

The agreement to arbitrate

Having determined to mandate arbitration as the basis for dispute resolution in the agreement drafted for parties, consideration should be given to the key components of the arbitration clause. The first (and imperative) goal is for it to be workable and capable of being enforced should the need arise. From this requirement, there are a myriad of choices to be made by the well-informed practitioner.

As a minimum there needs to be a clear process for the appointment of the arbitrator (or arbitrators). An odd number of decision-makers should be catered for in the arbitral clause. In many family law cases the selection of one arbitrator would be the norm. However, where the sums in question justify the additional cost, three arbitrators could be appointed. Appointment should usually be by mutual agreement of parties and in the event of disagreement between them on who to appoint, an appointing authority should be empowered by the arbitration agreement to select the arbitrator. It is a matter for parties to determine who should appoint the arbitrator in the event of disagreement as to selection, but many organisations are well placed to provide such an appointment service. The starting point when drafting an appointing authority into the clause could be a nominated office bearer at FLAGS (in a Scottish arbitration) or the law society or arbitration centre of the relevant jurisdiction.

If three arbitrators are prescribed, it is often the case that each party will be able to select their own arbitrator and a presiding arbitrator will be selected by the two party appointed arbitrators.

The scope of disputes covered by the arbitration clause should be clear and generally drafted as widely as possible to avoid enforceability issues.

The substantive law governing the rights and duties of parties under their agreement should be specified. This law will apply to how the agreement is interpreted.

The arbitral clause should make clear the seat of the arbitration. This is important as it determines the procedural law governing the arbitration. The absence of such provision may lead to argument over which law applies and thus lead to unnecessary delay and expense with court proceedings required to determine the point before commencement of arbitration.

Consideration should be given to other provisions such as the language of the arbitration, whether the arbitration proceeds on an ad hoc basis or an institutional basis (under the auspices of a recognised arbitration centre such as for example the Scottish Arbitration Centre, or the London Court of International Arbitration), and what rules for conducting the arbitration will be adopted, to name but a few.

The scope of how to draft the optimal arbitration clause in the agreement between parties is beyond the scope of this book (and is in any event fact-centric) but the IBA Guidelines for Drafting International Arbitration Clauses (2010) provides a useful discussion of the key elements for framing a well drafted arbitration clause.

Sources of Arbitral Rules

Arbitrations seated in Scotland are governed by the Arbitration (Scotland) Act 2010. Those seated in England and Wales (and Northern Ireland) are governed by the Arbitration Act 1996 (which at the time of writing is the subject of a Parliamentary bill to amend it). Both statutes provide a near comprehensive platform for arbitrations to operate in their respective jurisdictions. In Scotland the 2010 Act has a series of mandatory rules that cannot be over-ridden by the parties' arbitration agreement and a series of default rules that apply unless parties choose to contract out of them.[7]

Either statute, in addition to any institutional rules that the parties choose to adopt (or are required to adopt if they choose to proceed by way of institutional arbitration), are the main sources of arbitral rules that govern the arbitration process in a UK seated arbitration.

A set of arbitral rules has also been produced by FLAGS and is now in its third edition.[8]

---

[7] Schedule 1 (Scottish Arbitration Rules) to the Arbitration (Scotland) Act 2010

[8] FLAGS arbitration rules 2014 – 3rd edition

CHAPTER NINE

ENFORCEMENT

Although often considered at the end of the process of dispute resolution, enforcement is an issue that must be carefully contemplated by practitioners at the outset. No client will thank their adviser for a worthless (and expensively procured) legal decision. Consideration needs to be given to the issue of enforcement if one of the parties resides in another State, particularly so if that State does not recognise, or readily allow enforcement of, foreign court judgments or arbitral awards.

Court Judgements

Arrangements for recognition and enforcement of court judgments are dealt with within the UK through a statutory regime[9] and a well-recognised process exists for enforcement of Scottish decrees in England and Wales and court judgments from the rest of the UK being enforced in Scotland. The system of enforcement in the UK is a relatively uncomplicated and quick process. The position is less straightforward where recognition and enforcement is required outside the UK and has become more challenging following the departure of the UK from the European Union.

To have a judgment enforced abroad it must first be recognised in the jurisdiction in which it is sought to be enforced. Recognition is the process by which the national court confirms the foreign judgment and therefore makes it capable of being enforced in the jurisdiction of that

[9] Civil Jurisdiction and Judgements Act 1982

national court. Enforcement options available will then be dictated by the local law of the foreign jurisdiction.

The UK has entered many bilateral and multilateral treaties with other States, and it is therefore necessary to make enquiries into what arrangements exist. At a practical level ascertaining what reciprocal arrangements are in place through enquiry with the Foreign and Commonwealth Office in London can be a useful starting point for determination of enforcement routes. Sheriff officer firms may also provide useful practical information of how best to proceed where reciprocal arrangements exist.

Specific arrangements exist for the recovery of child maintenance from a parent living abroad or from a parent in the UK whose co-parent resides abroad. The UK has entered reciprocal enforcement arrangements for child maintenance with many countries.

It is unfortunately the position however that in many jurisdictions no route, or no clear route, exists for enforcing a court judgment to attach and recover assets of the other party in the foreign jurisdiction. In some situations, only a court decision of a higher court (the Court of Session in Scotland) is recognisable and enforceable and those of the sheriff court will not be recognised.

Ultimately if there is no route to enforce a judgment in the foreign jurisdiction, consideration should be given to commencement of proceedings there.

Arbitral Awards

A key advantage of international arbitration is enforceability.

There are several bilateral and multilateral Conventions governing recognition and enforcement of arbitral awards between States, but one Convention stands out from all others and is likely to be pertinent to most, if not all, family law arbitral awards. Most States (over 170) have signed this international Convention allowing recognition and enforcement of foreign arbitral awards[10]. A list of participating States is readily available from the website of the New York Arbitration Convention. Care should be taken to check any declaration or reservation made by the signatory State to properly understand any restrictions on its scope in the State concerned.

Grounds for resistance to recognition and enforcement under the New York Convention are limited. Provided the arbitral award arises from a valid arbitration agreement, proper notice of arbitration was given to the counterparty, the arbitrator was properly appointed, the operative decision in the award was within the arbitrator's jurisdiction and was made following respect for due process with parties having a fair opportunity to present their case, it should be recognised and enforced. Whilst there are grounds for resisting recognition and enforcement based on public policy it is, any pertinent cultural factors aside, difficult to see how that is apt to apply following family law arbitrations.

The existence of the New York Arbitration Convention and the active participation of States is at the heart of why international arbitration has flourished globally. The ability to readily enforce arbitral awards in many foreign jurisdictions underpins a key advantage of arbitration over litigation. The presence of an effective enforcement regime also results in greater voluntary compliance with arbitral awards.

As with foreign court judgements, a process is required to recognise the foreign arbitral award in the national courts of the foreign jurisdiction before enforcement steps can be undertaken. As with court judgements, enforcement options available for foreign arbitral awards will then be

[10] New York Convention on the Recognition and Enforcement of Foreign Arbitral Awards (1958)

dictated by the local law of the jurisdiction in which the award is sought to be enforced.

CHAPTER TEN

PARENTAL RIGHTS AND RESPONSIBILITIES

It is a commonly held misconception that if a child has been born in Scotland, and is living overseas, there arises an automatic right that a parent of that child can bring the child back to Scotland at any time, including if the parents of the child separate. That is certainly not the case.

The Children (Scotland) Act 1995 provides that the parents of a child have parental rights[11] and responsibilities[12]. A mother of a child has these automatically and a father of a child has these if he is named on the child's birth certificate[13] or was married to the child's mother at any time following the conception of the child[14]. The court can also remove a parent's parental rights and responsibilities or grant them as appropriate. The mother of a child can enter into an Agreement with the father, conferring parental rights and responsibilities on him, provided her own parental rights and responsibilities have not been removed by the court[15].

One such parental right is the right to determine matters pertaining to the residence of the child. If both parents agree that the child should

---

11 Children (Scotland) Act 1995, section 2

12 Children (Scotland) Act 1995, section 1

13 Children (Scotland) Act as amended by Family Law (Scotland) Act 2006, section 23

14 Children (Scotland) Act 1995, section 3

15 Children (Scotland) Act 1995, section 4

return to Scotland from overseas, it is of course within their rights as the child's parents to make that decision. In the event, however, that one parent wants the child to return to Scotland and the other parent does not agree that it is in the child's best interests for him or her to do so, there could follow a lengthy battle either in or out of the court to determine the issue. Unsurprisingly, there are numerous cases where a child's place of residence in the longer term is contested. In such cases, a court will require to decide where the child ought to live. The first matter to be determined though is "which court?"

Rarely should a client be advised to jump on a plane and return to Scotland with their child where the consent of the child's other parent has not been secured in advance. The courts in Scotland regularly hear cases brought by parents from other jurisdictions who make applications for the return of their children to the country where they usually live, known as the country of their "habitual residence" (see Chapter Twenty). These actions are brought when children have been removed unlawfully by a parent to Scotland or retained here in breach of the other parent's right of custody.

CHAPTER ELEVEN

THE HAGUE CONVENTION

When faced with a case involving the wrongful removal of a child the first port of call for legal advisors should always be the Hague Convention on the Civil Aspects of International Chid Abduction (hereinafter referred to as "The Hague Convention" or "the Convention") which has the force of law in the United Kingdom by virtue of the Child Abduction and Custody Act 1985. The Hague Convention is an international treaty which was signed in the Hague, Netherlands on 25th October 1980 and came into force on 1st December 1983. The text of the Hague Convention is broken down into numbered "Articles" for ease of reference. Signatories to the Convention are called "member states".

The primary purpose of the Convention is to protect children from the harmful effects of international abduction by a parent. It does this by facilitating the swift return of children who are removed from one member state to another without the consent of both parents. The rationale behind returning the child to its place of habitual residence is that by doing so the child is being returned to the country with which he or she has the closest connection. That country ought, therefore, to be best placed to make important decisions concerning the child's welfare. It also sets out to ensure that rights of access and custody under the law of one contracting state are respected in another contracting state[16]. Its provisions apply to children under the age of 16 years[17]. Once a child reaches the age of 16 the provisions of the Convention no longer apply.

[16] Hague Convention, Article 1

[17] Hague Convention, Article 4

There have been numerous changes to the member states since the 1980s. At the time of writing, there are 103 member states. As well as the general ethos behind the Convention as stated above, the Convention also requires that each member state puts in place practical measures to achieve the purpose of the Convention. Each member state is required to set up a Central Authority which is to be the main point of contact for both parents and the governments of other member states involved in abduction cases[18]. The purpose of the Central Authority[19] is to assist with the location of abducted children and to promote amicable solutions to parental abduction cases which, where appropriate, will include the safe return of children to their place of habitual residence. There are often formalities associated with lodging documents from foreign countries in courts. Any documents submitted to the Central Authority are admissible in the courts of all member states without such formalities in each individua member state having to be adhered to. The Central Authority involved in a child abduction case will be required to exchange any information they have received with the Central Authority in the other member state involved in the case. Cases brought under the Hague Convention move quickly. It is the expectation that a decision regarding whether the child is to be permitted to stay or will be returned will be reached within 6 weeks of the application being lodged. If this deadline is not met, the Central authority of the other member state has the right to request a note stating the reasons for the delay[20] .

It is important to note that that the parent seeking the return of a child need not be in possession of a residence order in respect of the child or have had the child living with them), in order to prove that their custodial rights were violated when the child was taken from his or her place of habitual residence. The Convention allows an application for the return of the child to be made providing that the parent has sufficient

[18] Hague Convention, Article 6

[19] Hague Convention, Article 7

[20] Hague Convention, Article 11

jurisdiction to proceed in the country from which the child was removed. In some cases, therefore, proof of parenthood or marriage will be sufficient. If a Scottish child were wrongfully removed from the United Kingdom the parent seeking the return of the child would not require a residence order to invoke the protection of the Hague Convention. Demonstrating that her or she has parental rights in respect of the child[21] gives them the right to seek the return of the child to the United Kingdom. Whether a child should be returned to his or her place of habitual residence or remain in the country to which he or she has been removed will not be determined by the immigration status of nationality of the child, nor of his parents.

Before the provisions of the Hague Convention can be invoked, however, there is one crucial condition which must be satisfied: both the country from which the child has been removed and one the child has been taken to must be signatories to the Convention. Once the child has been returned to his or her country of habitual residence it is then for the court of that country to determine whether the child ought to remain in that country in the longer term or if they should be permitted to relocate. In most jurisdictions the conduct of both parents will be considered and therefore the actions of the parent who removed the child without consent will be scrutinised by the court. It is unlikely that they will be viewed favourably. A better approach is to make an application to the court for removal of the child before attempting to relocate, as we will discover in later chapters.

The country from which the child was removed is recognised as being his or her country of "habitual residence". The concept of "habitual residence" is a matter of fact. (see Chapter Twenty)

If a child has been lawfully moved between member states habitual residence will move to the new state (and with it, the jurisdiction of the court to determine future contact/residence disputes) after a period of

[21] Children (Scotland) Act 1985, section 2

three months has elapsed since they arrived there. If a child has been moved unlawfully, however, jurisdiction will only shift to the new state if either (a) the other parent consents to the child's removal to or retention in the new state or (b) the other parent has been aware that the child has been living in that specific member state for a period of one year and has done nothing to disrupt that arrangement. It must also be demonstrated that the child is now settled in his or her new environment, failing which, the court could still order that the chid be returned[22]. A year may sound like a long period of time but parents abducting a child rarely leave a forwarding address. It may take the parent who has been left behind several months to find out which country the child has been brought to and even longer to pinpoint their exact location.

If neither of these defences apply, however, there is a third element which can be looked at when determining if a child ought to be returned: the views of the chid.

Article 13

There are, however, situations in which children will not be returned to their country of habitual residence even if that country is a member state of the Hague Convention. This is covered by Article 13 of the Convention. Article 13 is broken down into two paragraphs covering very different scenarios.

Paragraph (a) states that a child may not be returned if the parent seeking the return of the child was not exercising their custody rights at the time of removal or retention, or had consented to or subsequently acquiesced in the removal or retention. This covers the situation where a parent who had not had any involvement with the child's life attempts to prevent the child from relocating with their other parent. Some parents choose not to see their children, others have the right to contact with the child

22 Hague Convention, Article 12

removed by a court. For the purposes of this Article it makes no difference whether a parent has been removed from the child's life voluntarily or otherwise. This Article also prevents the return of a child if his or her parent previously consented to the removal of the child but revoked that consent after the child has relocated – whether because they had a genuine change of heart or purely out of malice.

The second paragraph of the Article, paragraph (b), is, however, perhaps the more important of the two from a child protection point of view. A member state may refuse to return of a child if "there is a grave risk that his or her return would expose the child to physical or psychological harm or otherwise place the child in an intolerable situation". The test is high. The threat facing the child must be real; it cannot be a perceived threat. The threat must also be against the child. This was examined in the Inner House case of *AD v SD*[23]. This case concerned a mother, SD, who was a Scottish and US citizen.

She married a US citizen, AD, and moved to Illinois, USA. The couple had two children. In June 2022, AD and the children travelled to Scotland for a holiday. They did so with AD's consent. They failed to return on a flight which had been booked for August 2022. SD justified this on the basis that she feared for her own safety and the safety of the children should they be forced to return to Illinois. It was accepted that children were habitually resident in Illinois and had therefor been wrongfully retained in terms of the Convention.

First AD raised proceedings in the US for dissolution of the marriage. In the context of that action he sought ancillary orders including an order which would have resulted in the children spending the majority of their time with him. He subsequently also sought an emergency order seeking the return of the children to Illinois under the Convention.

---

23 *AD v SD* [2023] CSIH 17

The Illinois court found that SD had abducted the children and ordered their return. Still AD failed to return the children to Illinois. In October 2022 AD raised a petition in Scotland under the Convention for return of the children. Whilst the Outer house sympathised with SD and accepted that there was evidence that text messages sent be AD to SD amounted to psychological, physical, sexual and financial abuse there was no suggestion that the children would suffer any harm and accordingly the children ought to be returned to Illinois. SD appealed to the Inner House. On appeal Lady Wise indicated that the court ought to look at the nature and severity of the risk to SD and should consider whether and to what extent that would impact upon the children. If there is a grave risk of the children being in an intolerable situation as a result of the mother's suffering, that may be sufficient[24]. What would happen if the children returned with her to Illinois ought to be considered. How would SD's anxieties impact upon the children? A child ought not to be returned if the impact of the abuse suffered by their parent would cause them to be placed in an intolerable situation[25] . (The Inner House overturned the decision of the Outer House and the children were not returned.

Article 13 of the Convention states that the court "may also refuse to order the return of the child if it finds that the child objects to being returned and has attained an age and degree of maturity at which it is appropriate to take account of its views".

It is important to note, however, that this Article says "may" refuse to grant the order to return the child. It does not state that it will not do so. Whether or not the child is to be returned is a matter of discretion for the court.

There is no minimum age at which a child can be deemed as being sufficiently mature to form a view. Each child will be considered on an

24 *Re E* [2012] 1 AC 144

25 *Re S* (a child) (Abduction: Rights of Custody) [2012] 2 AC 257].

individual basis. By way of example, in the case of *Blondin v Dubois*[26] a child aged 8 was deemed to be sufficiently mature to have their views considered by the court.

In this case, two children, aged 6 and 2, had lived in France throughout their lives. Their mother took them from France to the US without the father's (B's) consent. The father made an application to the court for their return. His application was refused. The French authorities then indicated that if the children were returned to France, protective measures would be put in place. The appeal was allowed. The case was remitted to the District Court to try to ascertain some way forward which would allow a return of the children whilst ensuring they were protected. The mother would be entitled to social security support. The father agreed to support them financially whist undertaking not to attempt to contact them until the French courts had considered whether contact was appropriate. The District Court again declined to return the children. The father appealed again.

The return was ultimately refused, based primarily on an Article 13 (b) argument, that being that there was grave risk that returning the children would subject them to harm owing to the violence they had witnessed their father perpetrate against their mother. During the case, however, the views of the children were sought and considered by the court. By this time the eldest (M) was 8 years old. As part of its judgment, the appeal court found that the court had not erred in finding that a child as young as 8 was of sufficient maturity to object to the return: "*B. does not argue that M. is immature for her age; rather, he simply questions whether any eight year-old is old enough for its views to be considered, and he observes that she is not as mature as a 12- or 13-year-old. This argument lacks merit. To accept it we would have to conclude that under the Convention, as a matter of law, an eight-year-old is too young for her views to be taken into account. We decline to do so, as this would read into the Convention an age limit that its own framers were unwilling to articulate as a general rule.*". It

26 *Blondin v Dubois* 238 F 3d 153 (2nd Cir 2001)]

should therefore be accepted that the Convention has purposely been drafted with no specific age in mind to enable a child's views to be considered by the court and his or her maturity determined by the court on a case-by-case basis.

That being said, however, the child's views in such a case should not simply be taken as read. Analysis of the views and how the child came to form them should be carried out. For example, was the child influenced by either parent or by another family member? This was examined in the case of *Cameron v Cameron (No 2)*[27]. This case concerned two girls, aged 5 and 7 who were born and brought up in Scotland. They then went to live with their father in France by agreement. On visiting the UK for contact, they were then retained in Scotland by their mother, without their father's consent. The father petitioned for their return. The court considered that although the eldest child had not been "tutored" in what to say when asked to provide her views regarding whether she should be returned to France or not, she may feel compelled to say things which please those family members presently closest to her. It concluded that she would be old enough to express a view, she may not be of sufficient maturity to present an objection as to the matter of return.

This all amounts to a "gateway" test. If satisfied that the child is sufficiently mature to give a view and he child actually wishes to provide one, the court can (if it believes the child's views are their own and they have not been influenced by an adult) take those views into account and use its discretion not to order the return of the child. The court can, however, choose to ignore the views expressed by the child and thereafter order their return to their country of habitual residence.

One interesting quirk though is that the child must express a view not to return to the country from which he or she came. Stating that they do not wish to return to their other parent is insufficient reason for the court to consider allowing the children to remain in the country to which they

---

[27] *Cameron v Cameron (No 2)* (1997) SLT 206

have been removed. If it is the other parent which the child has an aversion to living with, they could be returned to the country they came from but live independently from the other parent.

CHAPTER TWELVE

RELOCATING WITH CHILDREN: "SHARED PARENTAL INTENTION"

The concept of "shared parental intention" is one which causes headaches for family lawyers in various jurisdiction. It is interesting to note that is not an element to be considered while considering a child's place of habitual residence. The concept is best explained by looking at the facts of this case-

AR v RN[28]

This 2015 decision of the Supreme Court in this case has caused significant challenges for family lawyers, particularly those working within the field of child abduction. The majority of countries across Europe have the concept of "habitual residence" at their centre when dealing with the relocation of children. The Supreme Court unanimously dismissed the appeal of a father in this case and accordingly most litigators regardless of where they are based, should pay attention to this decision of the Inner House which held that "shared parental intention" was not an essential element in the alteration of a child's habitual residence.

Prior to this decision, it had been the readily accepted view of parents and lawyers alike, that the consent of both parents would be required in

28 *AR v RN* [2015] UKSC 35

order to change the habitual residence of a child, if both parents had parental rights and responsibilities in respect of that child. This case goes against that view in its entirety.

As indicated in previous chapters, parental rights includes the right to determine where a child lives. Although parental rights can be exercised by one parent without the consent of the other, this is subject to a prohibition against removal of a child from the United Kingdom without the consent of the other parent. It would then seem reasonable to presume that a child's habitual residence could not be altered without both parents agreeing to the change in advance. The Supreme Court disagreed. Instead, it emphasised the importance of the factual position relating to a child's habitual residence. It concluded that "stability of residence" was the determining factor in assessing where the child is habitually resident.

The decision in this case is hugely important for all parents who are considering living and working abroad. It means that, a child's habitual residence might shift to the country to which he or she has relocated without that being the intention of either parent.

The case concerned the arrangements for two young children who were born in France; the eldest in August 2010 and youngest in June 2013. Their mother was British/Canadian and their father was French. The family had lived together in France until shortly after the birth of the second child. In July 2013 the children moved to Scotland with their mother during her maternity leave. The children's father consented to this arrangement for an agreed period of twelve months. In November 2013 the mother discovered that the father had been unfaithful and decided to end their marriage. She then decided that she would not be returning with the children to France and raised residence proceedings in Scotland. The father responded by serving a Hague Convention Petition upon the mother seeking the return of the children to France. The basis of the Petition was that the mother's residence proceedings in Scotland amounted to her "unlawfully retaining" the children in Scotland in breach of the father's right of custody.

The pivotal issue was whether the children were still "habitually resident" in France or had transferred their place of habitual residence to Scotland at the point when their mother raised residence proceedings in Scotland. The case was raised just four months after they had left France for an agreed 12 -month period. If the children were no longer habitually resident on France, their father could not invoke the protections of the Convention.

At first instance Lord Uist concluded that the children had retained their habitual residence in France. He based that on his view that it was central to his decision whether- or- not there was a "joint intention" on the part of both parents to relocate permanently to Scotland. He decided that the absence of joint parental intention in this case was pivotal and therefore reached the conclusion that the children had remained habitually residence in France. Accordingly, the father could rely upon the protection of the Hague Convention.

However, the Inner House overturned that decision and the Inner House's decision was upheld unanimously by the Supreme Court. It was decided that the children's residence in Scotland had the requisite degree of "stability" for habitual residence to have shifted. This was held, despite the fact that the initial intention of both parents was that the children should reside in Scotland for a fixed and limited period of 12 months. The Court concluded that after only four months their life had the "necessary quality of stability" for them to have acquired a new habitual residence in Scotland. The father's right to rely upon the protection of the Hague Convention was lost and any contact or residence dispute relating to the children would take place in Scotland.

This decision makes it clear that irrespective of parental intention, and irrespective of whether-or-not there is an agreement that children should live in another country for only a short and fixed period of time their habitual residence could shift to the new country of residence.

CHAPTER THIRTEEN

THE WELFARE PRINCIPLE

The Hague Convention's main focus is not about the welfare of the child. For those practicing family law in Scotland, this seems very odd as this is of course the Court's only concern in child law cases here. (It is generally accepted that countries which are signatories to the Hague Convention have sufficiently mature judicial systems to deal with the welfare of the children who reside within their borders and that accordingly the "Welfare principle" is not a relevant consideration when looking solely at questions concerning jurisdiction. The legal systems of Hague Convention member states can be trusted to properly determine matters relating to children. It is also accepted that the best place to decide matters of welfare is the place where the child has been habitually resident and not the country to which the child has been abducted or in which the child is unlawfully retained, on the basis that the child has little connection with that country.

It is more likely that the Scottish courts will more readily accept jurisdiction if the child's place of habitual residence is not a signatory to the Hague Convention. The rationale behind this is that the legal systems in said countries are likely to be less well developed and consequently will be less well equipped to make decisions which will adequately protect the welfare of a child. Cultural differences could also lead to concern that one or other parent would not receive a fair hearing in some non-convention countries. Local customs and accepted practices in society may prevent it. For example, in some countries it is the norm for young children to always remain with their mother where older children may automatically reside with the parent with whom they share their gender. No other matters may be considered which could lead to outcomes which are detrimental to the child's welfare.

The child's welfare only becomes a live issue if it is determined that the Scottish courts are prepared to accept jurisdiction in a case. Only then, will the courts in Scotland make a determination as to where the child should live both in the interim and in the longer term. It is worth remembering that it is not inevitable that the child will be allowed to remain in Scotland. Parents ought to be prepared for the possibility that the Scottish court may still determine that the child's interests are best served by them being returned overseas after giving the case full consideration.

If a successful application under the Hague Convention has not been made and the Scottish Courts are prepared to accept jurisdiction in a case, the court will be required to look at a whole host of different elements before determining the country in which a child should ultimately live. In Scotland the overarching principle in cases which involve decisions regarding the arrangements for children is the "welfare principle". This is set out in Section 11 (7) (3) of the Children (Scotland) Act 1995 which states:-

> *"in considering whether or not to make an order under subsection (1) above and what order to make, the court—*
>
> *(a) shall regard the welfare of the child concerned as its paramount consideration and shall not make any such order unless it considers that it would be better for the child that the order be made than that none should be made at all"*
>
> *and*
>
> *(b) "taking account of the child's age and maturity, shall so far as practicable—*
>
> *(i) give him an opportunity to indicate whether he wishes to express his views;*

> *(ii) if he does so wish, give him an opportunity to express them; and*
>
> *(iii) have regard to such views as he may express".*

This provision contains some extremely important concepts which require to be considered in more detail.

1. The welfare of the child is to be the court's paramount consideration. It is not the role of the court to attempt to find a compromise which falls somewhere between the positions put forward by each of the child's parents. The court will not attempt to appease either parent. Children cannot be split in two and ought not be required to live a transient life, ricocheting across the world, in order to accommodate the living arrangements favoured by their parents. The sole function of the Court is to ensure that the child's welfare has been protected. The Court is not obliged to make any order at all. The law in fact goes further than that and says that a court should not make an order unless it is satisfied that do so would be better for the child than failing to make an order. What this means in practical terms is that it is for the parent seeking to depart from the status quo to persuade the court that the current arrangements are not in the child's best interests and that an alternative arrangement would be better for the child.

2. The court should (if practicable) ascertain the views of the child who is the subject of the dispute. This concept alone can cause difficulties.

CHAPTER FOURTEEN

VIEWS OF CHILDREN

In Scotland, there is no set age at which a child is deemed mature enough to express a view in cases relating to their welfare. All children have the right to do so. Some children will be able to provide the court with a well thought out and articulate opinion on what they would like the outcome of the dispute to be. Other children, of the same age will struggle to do so. Once the views of the child are made known to the court, it is for the Sheriff or Judge to determine how much weight ought to be given to those views. This will largely be dependent on the child's age and his or her level of maturity. It is worth noting however, that a child's views are not determinative. Even the views of an older child will not necessarily align with the decision which is ultimately made by the court. The child's views are merely one of a number of elements the court must consider when determining the outcome of a case. The other matters to be considered are outlined in Chapter Fifteen. The views of the child can be obtained in a number of ways.

In some cases, if the case is being dealt with in the Sheriff Court, the child will be invited to provide their views in writing by completing a form F9[29]. If the case is in the Court of Session the form is known as an F49.8A[30]. The form will set out the questions the child is being invited to answer using terminology which is age appropriate to the child and is set out in such a way as to be as straightforward and inviting to the child as possible. The questions on the form are tailored to each particular case

[29] OCR 33.7A

[30] any reference made to a form F9 in this book should be taken to also refer to Form F49.8A if the case is being litigated in the Court of Session

and must be approved by the court prior to it being sent to the child. Whilst this may be the least intrusive method for the child, there is concern that the views presented to the court on the form may not be entirely the child's own as except in the case of older children, there will likely require to be some form of adult supervision require by the child when filling out the paperwork. For this reason, it is good practice to send the F9 to the child's school where possible so that a trusted teacher or staff member can support the child in their completion of the form rather than allowing one of the parents to assist with that task. This should preserve neutrality insofar as is possible. Not only does this approach limit the scope for one parent to influence the material which the child inserts in the form, it also removes the potential for either parent to be accused of exerting any influence over the child. The other downside to ascertaining the child's views in this way is that there may be little explanation provided by the child as to why they have come the view they present to the court. Responses may be short and to the point with no background information provided, for example, "I want to live with Dad in Germany" or "I want to stary with Mum". On the face of it, these are clear views but with a little probing it may come to light that the child has formed these views based on facts which actually fly in the face of those outcomes being in their best interests. They may want to live in Germany with Dad because Dad does not impose any boundaries on them whereas Mum is actually the parent who provides a structured upbringing. The child may want to stay in Scotland with Mum because they are afraid that they will lose their pet if they relocate and not because they actually believe their mother to be the parent who supports and nurtures them. The court will simply be provided with whatever information the child wishes to provide without there being any opportunity to look behind that. There is no obligation on the chid to actually complete the form F9. They may choose not to provide a view or to send the form back stating that they want the adults to decide without their input.

There are, however, better ways of obtaining a more comprehensive version of the child's view. The court can order a report from a Child

Welfare Reporter. The Reporter will be an experienced Family Lawyer (not associated with those firms representing either party) who has been appointed by the Sheriff Principal in the Sheriffdom in which the action is brought. They are the "eyes and ears" of the court and will be given a clear remit from the court regarding which issues the court seeks to clarify. Whilst this process is undoubtedly more time consuming than sending out a Form F9 to the child, and there are cost implications associated with preparing the report, this approach generally brings about a much more satisfactory account of the child's views. As well as being able to accurately state the views of the child, the thought process behind those views can be made known to the court. It may be that the child has misunderstood some aspect of the case. Matters can be clarified and explored using this method. Younger children who cannot yet read and write to a high enough standard to complete forms can also make their views known. The reporter can take time to explain things in a manner which befits their level of maturity. A report from the Social Work department might be more appropriate where the family are known to the social work department given that the social worker will already know the background and will have established a rapport with the children.

CHAPTER FIFTEEN

OTHER CONSIDERATIONS FOR THE COURT IN CHILD RELOCATION CASES

The views of the child is just one element the court ought to consider when determining whether a child should live in Scotland or overseas. The court is obliged to take account of all the circumstances of the case. Whilst certainly not an exhaustive list, the court will require to consider a number of issues such as-

(a) Which parent was the primary carer of the child prior to the parents' separation. From a practical point of view, this parent is most used to meeting the day to day needs of the child. He or she will likely already have organised work and other commitments so as to allow them provide the care the child requires. The child is used to being in the care of this parent. They are used to living their everyday life with them and may consider them to be their "safe place";

(b) The type of accommodation which is on offer both in Scotland and abroad. The court will examine whether the accommodation on offer in each location will meet the needs of the child. It's quality, size and location will all be scrutinised, as will the amenities in the local area. It is not a case of "biggest is best" though. Each parent will simply require to demonstrate that adequate accommodation is on offer in their location of choice.

(c) Any additional persons who would be living with the child in each location will also be a matter of interest for the court, such

as other family members or a new partner (and their children). The child's relationship with those persons will be considered to ensure that their presence promotes the welfare of the child;

(d) Whether there are any language barriers associated with the relocation. If the child is to move to Scotland and does not speak English, the will expect to be informed of what measures will be put in place to help the child to learn English (assuming they do not already do so) and will need information regarding how the child will be supported until such time as he or she is able to master the language;

(e) The schooling arrangements in both countries. If there are issues relating to which language the child is to be taught in it would be expected that parents would explore international schools and any other assistance which is on hand to avoid the child's education being derailed in the interests of the move.

(f) The ability of the respective parents to financially support the child in each location. It is important to note, however, that it does not necessarily follow that the child will live with the more affluent parent. The court must, however, be satisfied that whichever parent the child is to live with has the financial means to support him or her, taking account of any child aliment which would be due to be paid by the other parent;

(g) The support network available to each parent. This covers a wide range of persons such as relatives, friends, child-care, medical practitioners etc. Anyone who would have an involvement with the child or parent with whom they would live;

(h) The child's own support network. The court will examine whether the child has a strong friendship group in the country of his or her habitual residence and the Sheriff or Judge will want to know whether it is likely that the child will be able to build a similar network in Scotland. Some children are outgoing and building a new group of friends would be easy. Others would struggle and removing them from the network they have developed could cause them emotional damage.

(i) How contact with the other parent will be facilitated. A clear plan for how contact would operate ought to be made available to the court. The proposal will require to cover the practicalities surrounding contact, such as how often contact would take place, for how long each period of contact would last, what the travel arrangements would be and where the other parent and the child would stay during contact. A plan for meeting the costs associated with contact such as travel and accommodation costs should also be made available to the court. The court, if it sees fit, can make an order determining which parent is to meet the costs associated with contact or can divide the costs between them in any portion it deems reasonable, taking account of the resources of each parent.

Each case is, however, unique. The court has an obligation to consider all the circumstances of each case when making a determination. The evidential onus is on the parent seeking to relocate to establish that it is in the child's best interests to relocate[31])

[31] S v S 2012 FAM LR 32 at para10

CHAPTER SIXTEEN

RELOCATING FROM SCOTLAND TO OTHER COUNTRIES

Relocating with children is not one way traffic. There is a steady stream of parents who wish to take their child to live abroad, who do not have the consent of the other parent. Where both parents have parental responsibilities and rights in respect of the child the removal of a child who is habitually resident in Scotland outside of the United Kingdom is unlawful without either the consent of other parent or with a court order where the other parent does not consent[32]. This even applies to travel for the purposes of a holiday.

The advice to be tendered to a client seeking to relocate is therefore similar to those seeking to enter the United Kingdom- they should not be advised to take the child and flee. The outcome of that approach is likely to be that the child will be returned to Scotland for the Scottish courts to determine whether or not the child should be permitted to relocate (if they attempt to move to a Hague Convention member state). If an attempt to flee with the child has been made, however, the applicant will then be approaching matters from the unenviable position of the court having already formed a dim view of their actions. At the end of the day, whether a child should be permitted to relocate or not is a matter of discretion for the court. It is therefore wise to follow protocol and keep the ear of the court.

The parent seeking to relocate with the child should be encouraged to make an application to the court under section 11 (2) (e) of the Children

[32] Children (Scotland) Act 1995, section 2(3)

(Scotland) Act 1995, commonly referred to as a "specific issue order". This will allow the court to determine whether to grant permission for the child to be taken abroad to live with the parent making the application or whether the child requires to stay in Scotland.

Again, the court must determine what is in the child's best interests taking account of the welfare principal when making its decision. The matters to be considered remain the same as in cases where the Scottish courts are determining the residence of a child who has been brought to Scotland without consent. All the circumstances of the case are relevant and will be scrutinised by the court, including the reason for the proposed relocation. There is a lower prospect of success if the applicant parent cannot show some connection to the country where it is proposed they will relocate to with the child, such as having family there or there being a significant employment opportunity available to them. It should not be viewed as an opportunity to choose somewhere random to move to, for the sake of it. A good example of this can be found in the following case:-

MS v SS (2012) CSIH17

The case was an appeal to the Inner house of the court of Session.

The parties were formerly husband and wife. They had been separated for almost 4 years and been divorced since 2010. They had one child, B who was six years old and who lived with his mother, the Pursuer. The Pursuer had an older daughter from a previous relationship. Both parties were employed as senior management with major international companies

The parties had been relatively amicable and had worked together to make arrangements for B's care without the necessity for a court order. Both were described by the Sheriff at first instance as having a deep relationship with B. Regrettably that amicable relationship did not last. In May 2011 the Pursuer was offered a significantly promoted post at her employer's principal office in Houston, Texas. She had not applied for the position-the approach from her employer had come as a complete surprise. In the short term, she had been permitted to commence her duties from her current home. She had been forced to resign from her current position and that role had been filled by someone else. If, therefore, the promotion could not come into full force because she was unable to relocate, she would have been forced to seek alternative employment. That may have been locally or in another part of the UK. She was clear that she would not consider relocating to Houston without B.

The Sheriff hearing the case at first instance was left weighing up two different outcomes, both of which was unsatisfactory in its own way. Firstly, he considered the positives for B of a move to Houston:-

1. B's outgoing personality which made it easy for him to make friends;

2. B had already expressed an interest in visiting Houston where his elder sister had lived at a similar age;

3. B would be likely to enjoy a higher standard of living in Houston;

4. B would experience a new culture where his mother already had friends and where excellent domestic, medical educational and other facilities would be available to him;

5. B was at the optimum age for relocation as he was no longer an infant but had not developed his own friendships and activities to such a degree that he would struggle to leave them.

The main downside of the relocation was of course the impact that the move would have on B's relationship with his father. It was accepted that the relationship was very well-established and the question was whether with appropriate planning that closeness could be preserved

The Sheriff also considered how B might be affected if the relocation was allowed to take place. He realised that the old status quo had gone and could never be regained as the Pursuer had lost her employment. Tension had become a common feature between B's parents as opposed to the peaceable co-existence which had existed before. There was a risk that the Pursuer may not find alternative employment in the local area and it was recognised that any movement (even within the UK) would impact on the child's contact with his father.

The single biggest negative to the move, the Sheriff determined, was that the current contact arrangements between B and his father could not continue. The Defender was criticised, however, for failing to co-operate in devising what suitable contact arrangements might look like if the relocation went ahead. The Defender was found to be an over emotionally involved parent who failed to separate B's best interests from his own. The Pursuer, on the other hand, appeared to be able to see both sides of the argument. It was ultimately established that the Defender had a reasonable annual leave entitlement which would enable him to travel to Houston to visit B. Other forms of communication such as Skype and telephone contact could also take place. The Pursuer was praised for being willing to facilitate and to pay for extensive contact both in the US and in Scotland. The Sheriff decided to grant a residence order in favour of the Pursuer and to allow the child B to relocate to Houston with her. The Defender appealed the decision.

At appeal, reference was made to Lord Fraser in G v G (Minors: Custody Appeal) 1985[33] who stated:-

> *"In most of these cases there is no right answer. All practicable answers are to some extent unsatisfactory and therefore to some extent wrong, and the best that can be done is to find an answer that is reasonably satisfactory".*

---

[33] *G v G* (Minors:Custody Appeal) 1985 1WLR 647 at page 651

Lord Fraser is, of course correct. There is often no right answer in cases involving children; just two parents, both with their hearts firmly in the right place, trying to do the best thing for their child. At appeal, it was also stated that the court may not interfere unless it is satisfied that the judge at first instance has not merely preferred one imperfect solution over another alternative imperfect solution which the Court of Appeal might or would have adopted, but has exceeded the range of reasonable options available to the court. Or to put it another way, as stated by Lord Scarman in B v W[34] in 1979 "the court may not intervene unless it is satisfied either that the judge exercised his discretion upon a wrong principle or that the judge's decision being so plainly wrong, he exercised his discretion wrongly".

The court of appeal recognised that, "*It was, in the end, for the sheriff to evaluate all aspects of the evidence before him in judging where the child's best interests might be thought to lie.*" The findings or conclusions of a judge of fact, based on having heard evidence from witnesses, would not lightly be disturbed on appeal. The appeal was refused and B was allowed to relocate to Houston with his mother.

---

34 *B v W* (Wardship: Appeal) [1979] 1WLR 1041

CHAPTER SEVENTEEN

PREPARING YOUR CLIENT'S CHILD RELOCATION CASE

It can be difficult to prepare for relocation cases. On the one hand, the applicant parent requires to provide a sizeable amount of information to firstly the other parent to allow them to consider whether or not they will consent to the move. If consent is not provided, the same information will then require to be provided to the court to allow the court to make an informed decision about what is in the best interests of the child. Presenting a vague and ill thought-out case is unlikely to result in a successful outcome. On the other hand that same parent will be criticised if they are presenting their case to the court as if it is a *fait accompli*. The best approach would seem to be for the parent seeking to relocate with the child to have a properly thought-out plan, ready to be executed as soon as the court grants permission for the removal of the child. Clients should be advised that they ought not to commit to anything that cannot be undone until after the other parent or the court has consented to the relocation.

If an order for the removal of the child is granted, the court can then make an order detailing the exact date on which the child can be taken from Scotland if the parents cannot agree that themselves. A contact order regulating the child's contact with the parent who is remaining in Scotland can also be granted by the court if necessary.

One of the issues the parent seeking to relocate will require to consider is what they will do if permission to relocate with the child is denied. That parent can still choose to relocate if they wish but will have to do so without the child in tow. Will they leave Scotland without the child or choose to remain here? If they decide that they will still leave Scotland, the court will likely grant a residence order in favour of the other parent. It is therefore crucial that the parent seeking to relocate does not find themselves in a position where they are forced to leave Scotland without the child because they have put wheels in motion which cannot be reversed. The most common scenario would be terminating their existing contact of employment and accepting a new position prematurely.

The case law in this area has taken some time to develop. Whilst each application which is made to the court will be determined on its own merits, it is interesting to consider those cases which have gone before.

For a number of years, the leading authority was the English Court of Appeal decision in Payne v Payne[35]. The decision in this case was however, rather controversial. In England, like in Scotland, the welfare of the child was to be the paramount or primary consideration of court. The court in this case, however placed huge significance on the desires and aspirations of the parent who was seeking to relocate. That is completely at odds with how applications are viewed here in Scotland. The likely outcome of that approach was that any reasonable and carefully framed relocation applications were likely to be granted by the Court. The Court also considered the effect of the refusal of the application on the applicant parent's future and their psychological and emotional stability. Whilst these are serious issues they ought to only become relevant to an action for removal of a child if they then affect the parent's ability to care for the child, thus impacting upon the child's welfare. The Scottish Courts were far more cautious in their approach and placed little weight on the feelings of the parents. They instead focussed solely on the welfare of the child, resulting in fewer applications being granted.

---

[35] *Payne v Payne* 2001 EWCA Civ 166

CHAPTER EIGHTEEN

CASES OF INTEREST

The evolution of the Scottish approach can be seen by examining 3 key cases- M v M in 2012 followed by S v S again in 2012 and more recently in Donaldson v Donaldson in 2014.

The 2012 case of **M v M**[36] involved a mother who wanted to relocate from Scotland to England with her two children. She had a new partner and extended family there. The order in her favour was granted at first instance; that decision was upheld by the Sheriff Principal but overturned on appeal.

In determining the case, the court had regard to the decisions in the cases of Sanderson v McManus[37] and Osborne V Matthan[38]. Lord Emslie in delivering the opinion of the court stated at paragraph [9]:

> *"On the binding authority of the decision in Sanderson, it can in our opinion be said with confidence that the requirements contained within s.11(7) of the 1995 Act effectively preclude reliance on any presumptive rule or guideline tending to favour the wishes or interests of either parent. As Lord Caplan observed in Osborne V Matthan (No.2) 1998 S.C., P.704; 1998 S.L.T., P.1278: "...Scottish courts, in particular, have resisted the*

36 *M v M* 2012 SLT 428

37 *Sanderson v McManus* 1997 SC (HL) 55

38 *Osborne V Matthan* (No 2) 1998 SC 682

> *temptation to elevate the primacy of the parental claim into anything approaching a principle, far less a rule.*"

He went on to state that "Moreover, the weight to be given to such wishes or interests must, as with any other factor, be such weight as the court deems appropriate in the particular circumstances of an individual case. In the end, the welfare and best interests of the child or children concerned are paramount, and fall to be judged without any preconceived leaning in favour of the rights and interests of others".

With regard to the effect of refusing an order to allow relocation, at paragraph [12], it was said by the court:

> "*Common sense suggests that, in some cases at least, the denial of a residential parent's legitimate wish to relocate may be productive of resentment and frustration. ....Again, in some cases, such resentment and frustration may come to impact adversely on the wellbeing of the child or children concerned. But, ...such consequences are by no means inevitable and a universal assumption that they will follow, or indeed that the best interests of affected children will necessarily coincide with the wishes and interests of the residential parent, would appear to be misplaced.*"

At paragraph [53], it was said:

> "*We acknowledge, of course, that there might be cases in which significant – even dominant- weight would incidentally attach to the reasonable relocation plans of a residential parent........What matters, in this as in any other case, is that the welfare of the children must at all times be the paramount consideration, and that the wishes and interests of either parent must receive no greater weight than they truly deserve in the circumstances.*"

At para [57] in allowing the appeal and recalling the Specific Issue Order which had previously granted, the Court said:

> "*Should the defender's present application be renewed, then in our view, she must undertake the dual burden imposed by s.11(7) of the 1995 Act, of showing (i) that relocation would actually be in the best interests of the children and (ii) that, again from the children's perspective, it would be better for a specific Issue Order to made by the court than for no order to be made at all*".

The more recent case of **Donaldson v Donaldson**[39] is also a decision of the Inner House. This is a case where a mother wanted to relocate with her 5-year-old child to San Francisco. The Order in her favour was granted at first instance; the father appealed against that decision to the Inner House.

The court reiterated the approach taken in M v M; that the general approach in such cases is a "presumption free" approach.

In the end the appeal was refused as the high threshold for appellate intervention had not been met.

At paragraph [27], it was said:

> "*Since the decision of this court in the case of M v M, it has been clear that, on an issue of relocation, it is no part of our law that a judge requires to regard any particular factor as having greater weight than any other. It would, for instance, be wrong to proceed on the basis that there is a rule that the most crucial assessment required is as to the effect that a refusal of the relocation application will have on the applicant. This is often conveniently described as a "presumption free" approach; it*

[39] *Donaldson v Donaldson* 2014 Fam LR 126

> *accords with the court's duty to regard the welfare of the child as the paramount consideration. That is not to say that, in an individual case, there may not be features which are of particular importance when considering the welfare of the individual child concerned.....Much will depend on the facts of each case."*

The main points of principle which can be taken from these cases in relation to the determination of applications for relocation are:

(1) That such cases should not be determined by the application of any general guidelines as this tended to deflect the court's focus away from the welfare and best interests of the child and was inconsistent with the non-presumptive approach which has been laid down by the House of Lords in earlier case law.

(2) That the correct approach requires to be non-presumptive, should focus on what is in the best interests of the child and in particular no special weight should be attached to the wishes or interests of either parent, though such wishes can remain a factor to be given such weight as is appropriate.

(3) That it is not to say that the reasonable relocation plans and reasons of a parent seeking a relocation order will have no weight but rather will be a factor to be taken into account with other potentially strong countervailing factors in the case:

(4) That there is an evidential burden on the party who seeks to alter the status quo to furnish the court with material potentially capable of justifying the making of the relevant order. Once the court has been furnished with that material the burden is removed. There is no ongoing legal discrete burden on the party seeking the order for relocation.

CHAPTER NINETEEN

INTERNATIONAL CHILD ABDUCTION AFTER BREXIT

The 1980 Hague Convention on the Civil Aspects of International Child Abduction is thankfully not an EU instrument. Its status as an international convention was not in itself impacted by Brexit. It continues to provide valuable and effective remedies for parents whose children have been unlawfully abducted from the country of their habitual residence for as long as the UK remains a signatory.

However, by leaving the EU, the United Kingdom is no longer a signatory to the Laguno Convention. This convention seeks to clarify which national courts have jurisdiction in cross-border civil and commercial disputes. It also provides a framework to ensure that judgments taken in such disputes can be enforced across borders. The United Kingdom has applied to accede to the convention as an independent member now that it has left the European Union. All signatories to the convention would need to agree to this. At the time of writing it looks unlikely that it will happen as the European Union has recommended that member states refuse the UK's accession. Unless this is rectified, this will cause untold difficulties in cross-border family law disputes.

CHAPTER TWENTY

HABITUAL RESIDENCE

The expression 'habitual residence' has received judicial scrutiny in several legal contexts and the concept remains the same, regardless of whether it is being looked at in relation to a child or adult. There are added complexities when looking at it from a child's perspective and so it makes sense to look at that here. Where any of the principles considered also apply to adults, it can be presumed that it also be applied when determining an adult's habitual residence.

It is a common misconception that habitual residence is linked to domicile. The place of an individual's habitual residence is better described as being the place in which they live their day to day lives.

The concept can be broken down and explained as follows:-

(a) it is a question of fact which is based on the child being integrated into a social and family environment;

(b) parental intent is of interest but is not the only issue of relevance. It is the factors that are at the centre of a child's life that are of utmost importance, such as where they return home to each night and where they attend school. His or her nationality or any cultural ties to a particular place cannot be given greater weight at the expense of geographical matters. This is particularly true in older children whose integration into society is more likely to be entirely independent of their parents than younger children whose lives are more intrinsically linked to their parents.

(c) a child will usually move seamlessly from one habitual residence to another. From a practical perspective, this makes perfect sense- a child cannot be in two places at once. Over time, a child will disengage with one place and form a connection with another. The change may come about quickly, or take some time but at some point, a shift in habitual residence will occur. It would be rare for a child to have no habitual residence. In the event, however, that this is the case the earlier of the two potential places of habitual residence should be favoured by any court charged with determining the matter.

(d) a court must carry out a comparative evaluation of the old and new places of residence to determine which is the habitual residence (Re J (A Child) (Finland) (Habitual Residence)[40] .

(e) a child must have been physically present in a country to be habitually resident there. A child cannot, for example change his or her place of habitual residence based on the fact that his or her parent has relocated to a new place HR v KO[41].

The Supreme Court dealt with the question of habitual residence in some detail in the case of A (Children) (AP)[42] [2013] UKSC 60.

The child in this case was a 3 year-old boy (H. His parents had dual English and Pakistani nationality. Including H they had four children. The other 3 children had spent time living in Pakistan and England.). H had been born in Pakistan and lived there all his life. He had never been to England. The father was abusive to the mother. The mother required to flee the home. She was able to return to England from Pakistan, but

---

[40] *Re J* (A Child) (Finland) (Habitual Residence) [2017] EWCA Civ 80

[41] *HR v KO* C-512/17 CJEU. UD v XB Case C-393/18 PPU

[42] *A* (Children) (AP) [2013] UKSC 60

did not have the children's passports. She therefore required to leave the children in Pakistan with the father.

Parker J determined that all four children (H and his 3 siblings) were habitually resident in England. She rejected a suggestion that there was any agreement that the children should live in Pakistan. She determined that H (the 3 year-old) was habitually resident in England, based on the habitual residence of his mother.

An appeal was refused in respect of the three older children, but allowed in respect of H on the basis that it was not possible to acquire habitual residence without physical presence.

The mother appealed to the Supreme Court. The judgment contains a detailed analysis of the concept of "habitual residence" for the purposes of the Family Law Act 1986 and the Hague Convention.

In her judgement, Lady Hale quoted Lord Brandon in the leading English case on habitual residence under the Child Abduction Convention, Re J (A Minor) (Abduction: Custody Rights)[43]:

> *"The first point is that the expression 'habitually resident', as used in article 3 of the Convention, is nowhere defined. It follows, I think, that the expression is not to be treated as a term of art with some special meaning, but is rather to be understood according to the ordinary and natural meaning of the two words which it contains. The second point is that the question whether a person is or is not habitually resident in a specified country is a question of fact to be decided by reference to all the circumstances of any particular case."*

The court, however, rejected the idea of habitual residence being equivalent to one's "ordinary residence", stating that "the reference to

[43] *Re J* (A Minor) (Abduction: Custody Rights) [1990] 2 AC 562, 578

adopting an abode "voluntarily and for settled purposes" is not readily applicable to a child, who usually has little choice about where he lives and no settled purpose, other than survival, in living there. If this test is adopted, the focus inevitably shifts from the actual situation of the child to the intentions of his parents."[44]

The court also made it clear that as residence must be "habitual", it is not lost by temporary absence[45].

The habitual residence must not be temporary or intermittent, so evidence pointing to a degree of permanence is particularly helpful.

This was all summarised by Lady Hale at para 54:-

> *"Drawing the threads together, therefore:*
>
> *i) All are agreed that habitual residence is a question of fact and not a legal concept such as domicile. There is no legal rule akin to that whereby a child automatically takes the domicile of his parents.*
>
> *ii) It was the purpose of the 1986 Act[46] (Family Law Act 1986) to adopt a concept which was the same as that adopted in the Hague and European Conventions. The Regulation must also be interpreted consistently with those Conventions.*
>
> *iii) The test adopted by the European Court is "the place which reflects some degree of integration by the child in a social and family environment" in the country concerned. This*

44 Para 39

45 Para 43

46 Family Law Act 1986

depends upon numerous factors, including the reasons for the family's stay in the country in question.

iv) It is now unlikely that that test would produce any different results from that hitherto adopted in the English courts under the 1986 Act and the Hague Child Abduction Convention.

v) In my view, the test adopted by the European Court is preferable to that earlier adopted by the English courts, being focussed on the situation of the child, with the purposes and intentions of the parents being merely one of the relevant factors. The test derived from R v Barnet London Borough Council, ex p Shah[47] *should be abandoned when deciding the habitual residence of a child.*

vi) The social and family environment of an infant or young child is shared with those (whether parents or others) upon whom he is dependent. Hence it is necessary to assess the integration of that person or persons in the social and family environment of the country concerned.

vii) The essentially factual and individual nature of the inquiry should not be glossed with legal concepts which would produce a different result from that which the factual inquiry would produce.

As the Advocate General pointed out in para AG45 and the court confirmed in para 43 of Proceedings brought by A, it is possible that a child may have no country of habitual residence at a particular point in time.

---

47 *R v Barnet London Borough Council, ex p Shah* [1983] 2 A.C. 309

CHAPTER TWENTY-ONE

CONCLUSION

We conclude this book with a round-up of the key practical questions which may crop up when a client first contacts you from overseas:

- Encourage clients to seek legal advice early on: If your client is a Scot living abroad, they may find that there is a possibility of more than one country having jurisdiction to deal with their case. In that event, it is sensible for clients to seek, at an early stage, advice from a lawyer in each of the potential jurisdictions. It may be that one country's legal system will deal with matters more swiftly, whilst another may lead the client to achieve a better financial outcome, so it is worth making a determination on jurisdiction as soon as possible.

- Request the ingathering of paperwork urgently: Prior to any initial meeting, it may be helpful for clients to ingather useful paperwork. This may include their marriage certificate, the birth certificates of any children of the marriage and translations of each if necessary, as well as any financial information pertinent to the dispute at the relevant date and the children's passports.

- Manage expectations: Tempting though it may be for clients to pack a suitcase and hop on the nearest plane, it is imperative that they do not to do so until proper legal advice has first been tendered.

- If children are involved, there can be criminal or civil legal consequences associated with them being removed from certain jurisdictions without the consent of the other parent being sought first. Advice should be sought on any potential relocation prior to the children's upheaval.

- It is easier to deal with ingathering any paperwork before clients leave the family home and potentially exit to another jurisdiction.

- Clients may need to consider any immigration issues that may arise if they decide to leave the country in which they are living.

- Communication is key: Most lawyers are now prepared to conduct client meetings online where required (thank you, pandemic). Some formal documents can be signed remotely and the courts are able to conduct hearings online in certain cases. There ought not to be any barrier to obtaining advice in these circumstances. Most lawyers who deal regularly with international cases will be pleased to accommodate any difficulties clients may be having with time zones. Our job is to remind clients of the accessibility of the profession, even in cross-jurisdictional matters.

Silence is golden: Clients should be reminded not to 'tip off' their spouses that they are considering divorce proceedings, whilst living in a foreign jurisdiction. If they do so, they risk the possibility of their spouse raising proceedings in a competing jurisdiction. If the client's spouse raises proceedings in the meantime, these should not be responded to until the client has sought legal advice in their current jurisdiction and that of their country of domicile, with the intention of challenging jurisdiction.

Living overseas can present challenges for many clients. They will have new transport and education systems to navigate, a battle to avoid getting into the wrong side of the car, thinking they have negotiated a bargain price only to find they have made a significant error in their currency conversion...

With day-to-day life already somewhat daunting, it is little wonder that something as earth shattering as the prospect of going through a separation when abroad can seem like an overwhelming process for many. As family lawyers, we do what we can for our clients to assist them in turning chaos into order. A case with an international element presents diverse and exciting challenges, but with careful thought, and using your international connections, a way forward is there to be found.

'A Practical Guide to Confiscation and Restraint' by Narita Bahra QC, John Carl Townsend, David Winch
'A Practical Guide to the Law of Forests in Scotland' by Philip Buchan
'A Practical Guide to Health and Medical Cases in Immigration Law' by Rebecca Chapman & Miranda Butler
'A Practical Guide to Bad Character Evidence for Criminal Practitioners by Aparna Rao
'A Practical Guide to Extradition Law post-Brexit' by Myles Grandison et al
'A Practical Guide to Hoarding and Mental Health for Housing Lawyers' by Rachel Coyle
'A Practical Guide to Psychiatric Claims in Personal Injury – 2nd Edition' by Liam Ryan
'Stephens on Contractual Indemnities' by Richard Stephens
'A Practical Guide to the EU Succession Regulation' by Richard Frimston
'A Practical Guide to Solicitor and Client Costs – 2nd Edition' by Robin Dunne
'Constructive Dismissal – Practice Pointers and Principles' by Benjimin Burgher
'A Practical Guide to Religion and Belief Discrimination Claims in the Workplace' by Kashif Ali
'A Practical Guide to the Law of Medical Treatment Decisions' by Ben Troke
'Fundamental Dishonesty and QOCS in Personal Injury Proceedings: Law and Practice' by Jake Rowley
'A Practical Guide to the Law in Relation to School Exclusions' by Charlotte Hadfield & Alice de Coverley
'A Practical Guide to Divorce for the Silver Separators' by Karin Walker
'The Right to be Forgotten – The Law and Practical Issues' by Melissa Stock
'A Practical Guide to Planning Law and Rights of Way in National Parks, the Broads and AONBs' by James Maurici QC, James Neill et al
'A Practical Guide to Election Law' by Tom Tabori
'A Practical Guide to the Law in Relation to Surrogacy' by Andrew Powell
'A Practical Guide to Claims Arising from Fatal Accidents – 2nd Edition' by James Patience
'A Practical Guide to the Ownership of Employee Inventions – From Entitlement to Compensation' by James Tumbridge & Ashley Roughton
'A Practical Guide to Asbestos Claims' by Jonathan Owen & Gareth McAloon

'A Practical Guide to Stamp Duty Land Tax in England and Northern Ireland' by Suzanne O'Hara
'A Practical Guide to the Law of Farming Partnerships' by Philip Whitcomb
'Covid-19, Homeworking and the Law – The Essential Guide to Employment and GDPR Issues' by Forbes Solicitors
'Covid-19 and Criminal Law – The Essential Guide' by Ramya Nagesh
'Covid-19 and Family Law in England and Wales – The Essential Guide' by Safda Mahmood
'A Practical Guide to the Law of Unlawful Eviction and Harassment – 2nd Edition' by Stephanie Lovegrove
'Covid-19, Brexit and the Law of Commercial Leases – The Essential Guide' by Mark Shelton
'A Practical Guide to Costs in Personal Injury Claims – 2nd Edition' by Matthew Hoe
'A Practical Guide to the General Data Protection Regulation (GDPR) – 2nd Edition' by Keith Markham
'Ellis on Credit Hire – Sixth Edition' by Aidan Ellis & Tim Kevan
'A Practical Guide to Working with Litigants in Person and McKenzie Friends in Family Cases' by Stuart Barlow
'Protecting Unregistered Brands: A Practical Guide to the Law of Passing Off' by Lorna Brazell
'A Practical Guide to Secondary Liability and Joint Enterprise Post-Jogee' by Joanne Cecil & James Mehigan
'A Practical Guide to the Pre-Action RTA Claims Protocol for Personal Injury Lawyers' by Antonia Ford
'A Practical Guide to Neighbour Disputes and the Law' by Alexander Walsh
'A Practical Guide to Forfeiture of Leases' by Mark Shelton
'A Practical Guide to Coercive Control for Legal Practitioners and Victims' by Rachel Horman
'A Practical Guide to the Law of Driverless Cars – Second Edition' by Alex Glassbrook, Emma Northey & Scarlett Milligan
'A Practical Guide to TOLATA Claims' by Greg Williams
'A Practical Guide to Elderly Law – 2nd Edition' by Justin Patten
'A Practical Guide to Responding to Housing Disrepair and Unfitness Claims' by Iain Wightwick

'A Practical Guide to the Law of Bullying and Harassment in the Workplace' by Philip Hyland
'How to Be a Freelance Solicitor: A Practical Guide to the SRA-Regulated Freelance Solicitor Model' by Paul Bennett
'A Practical Guide to Prison Injury Claims' by Malcolm Johnson
'A Practical Guide to the Small Claims Track – 2nd Edition' by Dominic Bright
'A Practical Guide to Advising Clients at the Police Station' by Colin Stephen McKeown-Beaumont
'A Practical Guide to Antisocial Behaviour Injunctions' by Iain Wightwick
'Practical Mediation: A Guide for Mediators, Advocates, Advisers, Lawyers, and Students in Civil, Commercial, Business, Property, Workplace, and Employment Cases' by Jonathan Dingle with John Sephton
'The Mini-Pupillage Workbook' by David Boyle
'A Practical Guide to Crofting Law' by Brian Inkster
'A Practical Guide to the Law of Domain Names and Cybersquatting' by Andrew Clemson
'A Practical Guide to the Law of Gender Pay Gap Reporting' by Harini Iyengar
'NHS Whistleblowing and the Law' by Joseph England
'Employment Law and the Gig Economy' by Nigel Mackay & Annie Powell
'A Practical Guide to Noise Induced Hearing Loss (NIHL) Claims' by Andrew Mckie, Ian Skeate, Gareth McAloon
'An Introduction to Beauty Negligence Claims – A Practical Guide for the Personal Injury Practitioner' by Greg Almond
'Intercompany Agreements for Transfer Pricing Compliance' by Paul Sutton
'Zen and the Art of Mediation' by Martin Plowman
'A Practical Guide to the SRA Principles, Individual and Law Firm Codes of Conduct 2019 – What Every Law Firm Needs to Know' by Paul Bennett
'A Practical Guide to Adoption for Family Lawyers' by Graham Pegg
'A Practical Guide to Industrial Disease Claims' by Andrew Mckie & Ian Skeate
'A Practical Guide to Redundancy' by Philip Hyland
'A Practical Guide to Vicarious Liability' by Mariel Irvine
'A Practical Guide to Applications for Landlord's Consent and Variation of Leases' by Mark Shelton
'A Practical Guide to Relief from Sanctions Post-Mitchell and Denton' by Peter Causton

'A Practical Guide to Equity Release for Advisors' by Paul Sams
'A Practical Guide to Financial Services Claims' by Chris Hegarty
'The Law of Houses in Multiple Occupation: A Practical Guide to HMO Proceedings' by Julian Hunt
'Occupiers, Highways and Defective Premises Claims: A Practical Guide Post-Jackson – 2nd Edition' by Andrew Mckie
'A Practical Guide to Financial Ombudsman Service Claims' by Adam Temple & Robert Scrivenor
'A Practical Guide to Running Housing Disrepair and Cavity Wall Claims: 2nd Edition' by Andrew Mckie & Ian Skeate
'A Practical Guide to Holiday Sickness Claims – 2nd Edition' by Andrew Mckie & Ian Skeate
'Arguments and Tactics for Personal Injury and Clinical Negligence Claims' by Dorian Williams
'A Practical Guide to Drone Law' by Rufus Ballaster, Andrew Firman, Eleanor Clot
'A Practical Guide to Compliance for Personal Injury Firms Working With Claims Management Companies' by Paul Bennett
'RTA Allegations of Fraud in a Post-Jackson Era: The Handbook – 2nd Edition' by Andrew Mckie
'RTA Personal Injury Claims: A Practical Guide Post-Jackson' by Andrew Mckie
'On Experts: CPR35 for Lawyers and Experts' by David Boyle
'An Introduction to Personal Injury Law' by David Boyle

These books and more are available to order online direct from the publisher at www.lawbriefpublishing.com, where you can also read free sample chapters. For any queries, contact us on 0844 587 2383 or mail@lawbriefpublishing.com.

Our books are also usually in stock at www.amazon.co.uk with free next day delivery for Prime members, and at good legal bookshops such as Wildy & Sons.

We are regularly launching new books in our series of practical day-to-day practitioners' guides. Visit our website and join our free newsletter to be kept informed and to receive special offers, free chapters, etc.

You can also follow us on Twitter at www.twitter.com/lawbriefpub.

www.ingramcontent.com/pod-product-compliance
Lightning Source LLC
LaVergne TN
LVHW022114200926
848481LV00003B/1169
9781913715823